WORKBOOK
FOR

CAN'T
HURT
ME

MASTER YOUR MIND AND DEFY THE ODDS

By

DAVID GOGGINS

PockeTBooks

Table of Contents

HOW TO USE THIS WORKBOOK

The book *Can't Hurt Me: Master Your Mind and Defy the Odds* by David Goggins is a book heavily loaded with wisdom for all readers no matter the sector you may find yourself.

The goal of this workbook is to fill you with wisdom, mental fortitude, strength, and the practical approach you need to defy all odds no matter what you see, how you feel, or what people are saying or have said to you. The only way this workbook can become effective in your life is for you to answer all the questions and, more importantly, answer them as sincerely as you can.

One great thing about this workbook is that if you haven't read the whole book, you can still understand some of the important points that can turn your life around. At the beginning of each chapter, you'll find that there are salient points to help you answer the questions for each chapter as you will also find these points useful when you're making decisions.

It is advised that you don't rush to answer the questions or create plans immediately you get this workbook. You need to think thoroughly and see clearly before you take any decision. Read the questions, pause to reflect, and read the questions again before you attempt the questions.

You need to evaluate yourself after you've answered the questions, and you've put the lessons you learned to practice. To do this, make an attempt to answer all the questions again after three months. You can decide to create follow up questions for yourself.

Remember that the key is to answer as honestly as you can, empathize with yourself and constructively criticize yourself in order to improve. If you find the questions too difficult, give yourself some time before you attempt it.

Make sure you answer all questions.

<u>INTRODUCTION</u>

The major point that runs through this workbook is that you need to come out of your comfort zone and stretch your limits and boundaries. You need to stretch your brain, your mind, discover and rediscover yourself.

You begin to sense and see the power of the mind and what it has to offer as well as what you're truly capable of. The mind is more powerful than you can imagine, and as humans, science tells us we haven't used up to half our minds.

The challenge is that we are naturally limited in the way we think, and this has also limited our capabilities. By reading the book, you can push beyond all limitations and explore the world so you can be who you're truly meant to be.

Denial is a great comfort zone. Seek out pain, be a partner with suffering as this will eventually make you pick yourself from the lowest part in life to become the best version of you. You have the potential to be much more.

Open your mind as you kiss failures goodbye as well as mediocrity, people's opinion, years of abuse, depression, and what others have said about you and step out as a strong man, strong woman, and an overcomer as you learn to master your mind.

CHAPTER 1: I SHOULD HAVE BEEN A STATISTIC

Here are some key points we learned in this chapter

Physical and emotional abuse in young kids negatively affects their young minds. If kids are exposed to violence and abuse consistently, it becomes their baseline.

Consistent violence and abuse put kids in fight or flight mode or a state suitable for danger alone because that is what you need to get out of trouble. However, it isn't the ideal state to be every time.

When abuse and violence becomes a norm in the life of kids, they grow up with a higher risk of clinical depression, obesity, heart diseases, cancer, alcoholism, drug abuse and they can inflict abuse on others too. The kids who grow up in an abusive household have a 53% probability of being arrested as a juvenile, and they have a 38% possibility of committing a violent crime as an adult.

Who you are or what you are determines who you will attract.

The mindset and help from a teacher can help kids who are struggling academically. The teacher needs to be involved and interested in the child and not focus only on productivity.

Whenever you're the only one of your kind, you're in danger of being pushed toward the margins, suspected and disregarded, bullied and mistreated by ignorant people.

Sometimes, the kids you think have a problem don't really have a problem. If you can listen to them and hear what they say, you'll notice they are really fine. It's the world around them they're reacting to.

Answer the following questions as sincerely as you can

1. The brain of kids grows and develops rapidly.
   True **or** False
2. Abuse has a wide range of effect on the minds of kids
   Yes **or** No
3. Abuse can lead to toxic stress in kids. True **or** False
4. Stress in kids can be easily managed when compared to meningitis or polio. True **or** False
5. Do you know anyone who went through childhood trauma, abuse, and violence? Yes **or** No
6. Is the person involved in drug abuse, alcoholism, or any other kind of crime? Yes **or** No
7. Who was your best teacher in school when you were a kid?

   _____
   _____

8. Why was the person your best teacher? Did the teacher give you attention, listen to you, believe in you, or put more effort into helping you? Mention them

   _____
   _____
   _____
   _____
   _____
   _____

9. What was the worst coping mechanism you ever used to bail yourself out in any situation? Was it cheating, lying, stealing? What was it? Pen it down

   _____
   _____
   _____

10. If you meet a kid who's going through what you went through as a child, what advice can you give? How can you help them?

_____

_____

_____

_____

_____

_____

11. What were the challenges and bad situations that happened to you when you were growing up? Was it bad neighbors, bad parenting, alcoholic parents, absent father, abandonment, were your parents into drug and substance abuse? Mention them

_____

_____

_____

_____

_____

_____

12. How did the situations in the previous question influence that you are as a person now? Did it make you someone who doesn't like families or someone who is into drug and substance abuse, or do you abuse your kids and partner?

_____

_____

_____

_____

_____

_____

13. Start journaling. I advise that you use a hard copy journal and pen because it's more therapeutic. However, you can opt for a soft copy and download a journaling app on your phone, tablet, or laptop. Write about the experiences that hurt you the most and the ones that still hurt. You may come up with a number of excuses why it wouldn't work, but tell yourself you

can do it. When you're done writing at the end of each day, share it with whoever you want.

14. Share your story with the world or anyone you desire to share it with. This means you can go on your social media pages, write a story about how your past or present circumstances challenged you to the depth of your soul. End the story with the hashtag, such as #badhand #canthurtme.

CHAPTER 2: TRUTH HURTS

Here are some key points we learned in this chapter

Choose the people around you wisely. Move with people who bring out the best in you. This doesn't mean you should become unaware of who they really are. Don't close your eyes to the signs that show you who the person really is. That's how you'll know if they are dangerous or calm and good.

Life is hard when you're alone. Don't stay alone if you have to, but if life happens and everyone around you leaves, brace yourself, and move on. You'll do just fine on your own than when you're with the wrong person.

Life happens; good things happen to good people just as bad things happen to good people. Never believe that you are bad or that you deserve to be sad all your life.

You don't need to live a hard life or thug life to make your point known or to be heard. This may affect your life in the worst possible way.

For real change to happen in you, be ready to give it all you've got and work your way out of the debris you're in. Build yourself from the inside out, and don't just change your wardrobe and looks to show everyone you've changed. Real and true change is challenging; be ready to work it out.

Unless you decide to make your life worthwhile, no one can make your life worthwhile. You have to deliberately decide to be a new person.

Don't cut corners or always look for the shortest route or escape out of any situation. You may end up regretting it at the end.

Get yourself an accountability mirror or something that makes you stay accountable to your goals. You need a positive attitude to go with it.

You need to be sincere with yourself if you want to progress in life. Tell yourself the truth and don't mince words. Life is short, and you don't have all the time you think you have. Hours and days can easily disappear or evaporate like creeks in the desert.

You're permitted to be hard and cruel to yourself if it will eventually make you better. This is because a thick skin is what you need to improve yourself in life.

Even when you decide to own your life and do your best to improve, don't expect life to be sweet and sassy with luck coming your way immediately. Life will still remain difficult even when you're at your best. You need to be consistent in giving your all and your best.

Learn to face your fears. Don't stifle your emotions, let it out, and breathe.

If someone makes fun of you or tries to bully you, they are the ones with the problem and the insecurity, not you. Don't let anyone force you out of what is yours, never agree to it.

Grow your confidence. Without it, you prioritize other people's opinions above yours, and you place too much value on what others say or do without evaluating their words.

Understand why you take the stance you do and why you do the things you do. Have a reason you believe in and don't just do things or say things because everyone is doing or saying it.

Don't be scared if you're the 'only' in any given situation or circumstance. Stand your ground and tell yourself the truth always. Live with purpose.

When you transcend a place in time that has challenged you to the core, it can feel like you've won a war but don't fall for that mirage. Your past, your deepest fears have a way of going dormant before springing back to life at double strength, so remain vigilant always.

Set goals, write them on post-it notes, and tag them on your accountability mirror or a place where it looks you right in the face.

No one has the right to stop you except you do.

Train yourself to seek out discomfort. Don't go for convenience as it wouldn't help you become strong. Be ready to fight yourself to become who you're meant to be.

Answer the following questions as sincerely as you can

1. Being tough and resilient helps you meet your goals.

   True **or** False

2. Knowledge sticks by learning, not transcription or memorization or repeat and recall. True **or** False

3. Personal accountability is the best gift you can give yourself. True **or** False

4. How was life difficult for you when you were growing up? What specific experiences do you remember?

   _____
   _____
   _____
   _____
   _____
   _____

5. Have you ever had to call yourself out in any situation when you were failing? Yes **or** No

6. Was there any form of progress after calling yourself out? Did you use your negativity as a fuel to propel you forward? Yes **or** No

7. What was the lowest you were in life? What was the situation like?

   _____
   _____

_____
_____
_____
_____

8. What made you scared while you were growing up? Were there specific situations that made you avoid doing things you loved or going to specific places? Were you bullied at a certain spot or embarrassed? What was it?

_____
_____
_____
_____
_____
_____

9. How did you get over such feelings and situations? How did you get over your fears?

_____
_____
_____
_____
_____
_____

10. Have you ever felt your past creeping up on you, making you feel bad, terrible, or the way you used to feel before you decided to get accountable? Yes **or** No
11. Can you explain the feeling and how you get over it?

_____
_____
_____
_____
_____
_____

12. Write out your goals, write them on post-it notes, get yourself an accountability mirror, which is a mirror you look into every morning and use it to get yourself accountable.

13. Write out your insecurities on your post-it notes. Write out all the things you need to do to get better in life. It doesn't matter if it is going back to school or losing weight. Make sure you write it so you can see it. Write out your plan for achieving such goals.

CHAPTER 3: THE IMPOSSIBLE TASK

Here are a few points we learned in this chapter

If you don't like or love you, nobody will do the same.

When faced with challenges, it is normal for your mind to challenge you with negativity and doubt. However, it's your decision to relax and not be moved by it.

Without dealing with your fears and insecurities, it will lead to all other black holes in your past. Never let fear dictate your future, or you'll live in regret within yourself for the rest of your life. Take charge of your destiny. No one may know, but deep in your heart and soul, you'll know, and it will always hunt you.

Don't always go for the easiest option or cut corners. The effect lingers in your mind. Endure the physical suffering to alleviate the mental suffering. Either way, you choose one suffering.

Not all physical and mental limitations are real so don't give up too soon

Answer the following questions as sincerely as you can

1. Trauma and failure affect the mind and weighs down on the soul. True **or** False
2. Courage and toughness is essential when dealing with the impossible True **or** False
3. Have you ever faced a challenge where you felt you gave up too soon? Yes **or** No
4. What was the challenge about?

_____
_____
_____
_____
_____
_____

5. Did you revisit the challenge? Yes **or** No
6. How did you pull through?

_____
_____
_____
_____
_____
_____

7. Describe your daily routine

_____
_____
_____
_____
_____
_____

8. Are there things that have become a norm and your comfort zone, but you know you need to break out of it. Is it losing weight or leaving the job you don't like? Mention them

_____
_____
_____
_____
_____
_____

9. What are the dreams you have, but you haven't been able to accomplish? Is it getting a new degree, going back to school, losing weight? Pen it down

_____
_____
_____
_____

_____

_____

10. What are the steps you need to take to meet up with each of your goals? Mention the steps and what you can do and how you can begin.

_____

_____

_____

_____

_____

_____

11. What are the few things that make you uncomfortable but will make you better and stronger eventually? Mention them and take pictures of yourself doing them and place them on your accountability mirror

_____

_____

_____

_____

_____

_____

12. Use the picture to tell your story on social media and use the hashtags   #discomfortzone   #pathofmostresistance #canthurtme #impossibletask

CHAPTER 4: TAKING SOULS

Here are a few points we learned in this chapter

When it feels like you can't hold to your goals or dreams, the best thing is to remind yourself of the reason you began in the first place. Your motive or purpose will see you through.

Before picking up any challenge or goal, remind yourself that it isn't going to be the easiest thing and tell yourself you'll never give up.

Everything in life is a mind game! Whenever we get swept under by life's dramas, large and small, we are forgetting that no matter how bad the pain gets, no matter how harrowing the torture, all bad things end.

Don't be too hard on yourself. Finding moments of laughter in pain and delirium will turn the entire melodramatic experience upside down for us. This is how to gain control of your emotions.

You need the right people around you to act as your support system. They can encourage you when you're down and help you move forward when you're at your lowest.

Taking souls concept is a ticket to finding your own reserve power and riding a second wind. It's a tool you call upon to win any competition or overcome any obstacle. It simply means gaining tactical advantage. It is an act that empowers you. To do this, understand your terrain, so you know when and where to push boundaries and when to fall in line.

Before you give up, think of how you would want to be remembered.

Answer the following questions as sincerely as you can

1. Suffering can be used to pick and peel layers till our minds are fit and strong. True **or** False

2. Giving your emotions and actions to others when pain is at its peak makes you forget that pain is a mind game.
   True **or** False
3. Do you have a support system? Do you have people who can encourage you when you don't feel up to it?
   Yes **or** No
4. Mention two of those people and how they've encouraged you in difficult times.

   _____

   _____

   _____

   _____

   _____

   _____

5. The best way to defeat a bully is to actually help them.
   True **or** False
6. What has been your tacking soul approach when someone above or ahead of you tried to bully you?

   _____

   _____

   _____

   _____

   _____

   _____

7. Think of the most challenging situation you've ever found yourself. Think of a worthy opponent. It can be a rude client, a coach, a boss, a competitor. Describe the situation

   _____

   _____

   _____

   _____

   _____

   _____

8. Think of a way to deal with the situation. It may be taking an exam, taking additional classes, writing out a proposal, giving more time to a task, or taking up a project. Do what you're supposed to do and think of a better way to come out on top of the situation.

_____

_____

_____

_____

_____

_____

9. When you come out on top, watch them see you achieve what you've done for yourself. Make sure their negativity is a fuel for you to get better. Write a post about it on social media using the hashtag #canthurtme #takingsouls

CHAPTER 5: ARMORED MIND

Here are a few things we learned in this chapter

Until you experience hardships like abuse and bullying, failures, and disappointments, your mind will remain soft and exposed.

If you choose to see yourself as a victim of circumstance into adulthood that callous will become resentment that protects you from the unfamiliar. This can make you too cautious and untrusting and angry at the world. This will make you fearful of change and hard to reach.

No matter the negative situations you find yourself, you must learn to always keep your heart open. This shows you're willing to move on and not give up.

Just as you can use your opponent's energy to gain an advantage, leaning on your calloused mind in the heat of battle can shift your thinking as well.

When you remember what you've been through and how that has strengthened your mindset, it can lift your brain out of a negative brain loop and help you bypass those weak, one-second impulses to give in so you can power through obstacles.

Leveraging on your calloused mind can help you fight through the pain and push your limits because accepting the pain and refusing to give up will engage your sympathetic nervous system, which shifts your hormonal flow.

Managing moments of pain that come with maximum effort by remembering what you've been through to get to that point in your life, you will be in a better position to persevere and choose fight over flight.

Answer the following questions as sincerely as you can

1. A negative experience can make your mind calloused, but you determine how calloused your mind will be.
    True **or** False
2. Indulging in negative self-talk wouldn't allow you to think of a way out when you're down and out. True **or** False
3. What hell week have you ever gone through? Is it getting a dream job, getting a degree, passing exams? What was it? Pen it down

_____

_____

_____

_____

_____

_____

4. What did you discover about yourself during those times?

_____

_____

_____

_____

_____

_____

5. What was the attitude from your superiors, supervisors, or bosses? How did it spur you on?

_____

_____

_____

_____

_____

_____

6. How did you manage the pain you felt during those periods?

_____

_____

_____
_____
_____
_____

7. Have you ever had a goal that you couldn't fully execute?
    Yes **or** No
8. What were the reasons why it wasn't executed? Was it lack of funds, lack of plans, a mental breakdown, or procrastination? Pen it down

_____
_____
_____
_____
_____

9. Tick the appropriate answer
*   Surviving difficulties makes you strong. True **or** False
*   Surviving challenges from superiors or bosses makes you calloused. True **or** False
*   Tolerating taunting and abusive words from your others makes your mind calloused. True **or** False
*   Giving room to doubt will allow it to run over and control you. True **or** False
*   Managing doubt helps you think of a way out. True **or** False
*   Taking charge of your fears and difficulties will barely help you get through life. True **or** False
*   It is important to master your mind. True **or** False
10. Before you sleep, write out a note to yourself. The aim of this writing is to help you get through the following day. Write a note to yourself, telling yourself what you've been through and how you understand. Write words of encouragement as well, and place it on your accountability mirror. Make sure that's the first thing you read when you wake up.

Here's an example: Ryan, you've been through a lot, you've lost loved ones, lost money, friends have betrayed you, you've been cold, hungry, lonely and sad but guess what? You're still standing. This means you are strong and have the ability to do more than you can imagine. Today is another day to face more challenges, and you'll come out on top of it. Don't give in, and don't give up. You will overcome. (Mention your personal challenges)

_____

_____

_____

_____

_____

_____

11. Open your mind and choose a new obstacle or a goal. Think of a way to overcome this obstacle or a new way to achieve the goal. Pen it down and work it out. Try it out and write a story about it on social media with the caption #canthurtme

_____

_____

_____

_____

_____

_____

CHAPTER 6: IT'S NOT ABOUT A TROPHY

Here are a few things we learned in this chapter

Sometimes you need to be real and speak up about how you truly feel for you to get help.

If you aren't prepared before you find yourself in challenging situations or if you allow your mind to remain undisciplined in an environment of intense suffering, the only answer you'll find is the one that will make it stop as fast as possible.

You gain a different self-knowledge when you're broken down to nothing, and you find more within only through going through challenges.

You need to keep going on even when you have the chance to quit. Don't let small wins make you feel fulfilled, rather let it push you to achieve more.

We need small accomplishments to fuel the big ones. Your small accomplishments kindle the big ones. They are like small fires that will eventually bring the forest down. Don't run after the big accomplishments without consistently gaining small wins.

Answer the following questions as sincerely as you can

1. Challenges prepare you for further challenges, and you can make decisions quickly. True **or** False
2. Overcoming challenges make you wiser. True **or** False
3. Endurance doesn't affect your capacity to withstand challenges. Yes **or** No
4. What were the small wins you achieved that propelled you to make more wins? Was it losing weight? Getting over a personal challenge? Meeting up with an important deadline? Write it down

_____
_____
_____
_____
_____
_____

5. How did it help you take greater challenges and make more wins?

_____
_____
_____
_____
_____
_____

6. How do you deal with what seems at intense pain? Is it by sleeping, drawing out plans to deal with the pain, looking through the pain, or thinking of a way you dealt with pain before? Mention them

_____
_____
_____
_____
_____
_____

7. Create your own cookie jar. It doesn't have to be a literal cookie jar but use something that can serve as one. Write out your personal achievement list and the obstacles you've endured and overcome. It doesn't have to be a very list, and remember there's nothing for you to feel shy or ashamed of if it isn't a long list. The list should also contain tasks you attempted more than once or twice before you overcame. It may be passing an exam, overcoming depression, overcoming struggles with opponents until you win.

_____
_____
_____
_____
_____
_____

8. Look at the obstacles in your way and compare it with the list containing tasks that you accomplished after attempting it two, three or more times. Draw out different plans to accomplish your goals.

_____
_____
_____
_____
_____
_____

9. Try out the plans until you have a breakthrough. When you do, write out a post or post pictures of your effort and accomplishment on social media using the hashtag #canthurtme #cookie jar

CHAPTER 7: THE MOST POWERFUL WEAPON

Here are a few things we learned in this chapter

Sometimes you may never know what you're capable of until you try. If you listen to your fears, your doubts, your body, and your loved ones, you may never get to try.

Try talking to people who have gone through what you've been through as they can give you tips that can help you move forward.

If you go through a challenging time and everyone around you can see it and comment on it, don't let it stop you from what you're doing but let it push you forward. Don't wallow in the negative comment by others.

It is only when you push beyond your pain and suffering and your perceived limitation that you're capable of accomplishing more, physically, and mentally both in endurance races and in life generally.

Continue to do things that will build your confidence.

The human body is like a stock car. We may look different on the outside, but under the hood, we all have huge reservoirs of potential and a governor impeding us from reaching our maximum velocity.

Our governor is buried deep in our minds, intertwined with our very identity. It knows what and who we love and hate; it reads our whole life story and forms the way we see ourselves and how we'd like to be seen. It's the software that delivers personalized feedback – in the form of pain and exhaustion but also fear and insecurity, and it uses all of that to encourage us to stop before we risk it all.

Most times, people give up after only putting in 40 percent of their maximum effort.

When you know you have more capacity for pain and tolerance, you can stretch yourself and let go of your identity and self-limiting stories that you've always told yourself. This is what pushes you from 40% to 60% and then to 80% and beyond before giving up: **this is the 40% rule**.

In life, almost nothing will turn out the way you want it to, and there will always be challenges and obstacles along the way. We will always be tempted to give up on our goals and dreams and sell our happiness short at some point. You'll know when you haven't given your all because you feel empty when you haven't tapped into your mind, soul, and heart.

You can't tap into your 60% right away, so the first blast of pain and fatigue is from your governor. Don't dialogue with it. Fatigue makes cowards of us all.

Sometimes your survival may depend on how much information you have. Get more information about the challenges you're facing and come up with a creative way to deal with your challenges or your obstacles. Research is important.

Remember the Goggins' law of nature: You'll be made fun of, you'll feel insecure, you may not be the best all the time, you may be the only black, white, Asian, Latino, gay, lesbian in any given situation, you'll feel alone sometimes but get over it.

Answer the following questions as sincerely as you can

1. For humans, our governor is buried deep in the brain and mind. True **or** False
2. The governor is the control of the body. True **or** False
3. When you feel like you've given all that is within you, you still have 60 percent in reserve to give. True **or** False
4. The only way to move beyond your calloused mind is to push beyond your daily output of 40%. True **or** False
5. Mention the top 10 things you're sure that you're capable of

_____

_____

_____

_____

_____

_____

_____

_____

_____

6. Mention the top 10 things you can't do, but you wish you could.

_____

_____

_____

_____

_____

_____

_____

_____

_____

7. What are the reasons why you can't do them?

_____

_____

_____

_____

_____

_____

8. Imagine you have a nephew, and he told you of the things he wished he could do, and he also gave you the reasons why you couldn't do it. What would you tell him?

_____

_____

_____

_____

_____

_____

9. Think of a particular challenge in your way and apply the 40% rule to it. Write out the steps and the part where you give up and then think of how you can push to 60%, 80%, and give more. Write it all out.

_____

_____

_____

_____

_____

_____

10. For every time you gave up when you were faced with an obstacle, what excuses or reasons did you give yourself? What did you tell yourself? That it wasn't worth it, it was too difficult, or you'll be fine without it? Mention them

_____

_____

_____

_____

_____

_____

11. Think about those excuses now and ask yourself if they were really genuine. Could you have stretched yourself some more? Yes **or** No

12. Will you be willing to go through these challenges again without giving up? Yes **or** No

13. Pick one of your current challenges. It could be getting a promotion at work or studying to pass an exam. Research on the different ways you can come out on top.

_____

_____

_____

_____

_____

_____

14. Write out your weaknesses and vulnerabilities and think about them too. How do you prepare for them, so it doesn't overwhelm you?

_____

_____

_____

_____

_____

_____

15. Go back to your cookie jar and remind yourself of all the things you've done. This will help you get through the tough times when you're feeling down and out. Pick one that inspires you and write out the story on social media using the hashtag #canthurtme

_____

_____

_____

_____

_____

_____

16. As you are overcoming your hurdles daily, write out a post on it on social media using the hashtag #canthurtme #the40percentrule #dontgetcomfortable

CHAPTER 8: TALENT NOT REQUIRED

Here are a few things we learned in this chapter

You need a strategy to win. Without this, it may be impossible for you not to fail. Your strategy is your vantage point and your intellectual advantage.

You never know who you are affecting. Do your best every time, and in every situation you find yourself.

Never rely on quick fixes or life hacks or simple steps. It may lead to small chances of success if you're lucky, but it wouldn't help you master yourself.

To master your mind, remove your governor. You'll have to become addicted to hard work because passion, obsession, and talent are only useful tools if you have the work ethic to back it up.

Evaluate your life in its totality! We all waste so much time doing unimportant things.

Analyze your schedule, kill your empty habits, burn out the unimportant things to find what is important, and maximize the time to what's important.

Make room to rest in between tasks. It can be sleeping or simply lying down. Switch off your TV, Smartphone, Computers, and other electronic gadgets.

Even when you're doing everything right, chaos will always be right at the corner. It's life, so be prepared!

Life will always be the most grueling endurance sport, and when you train hard, get uncomfortable, and callous your mind, you will become a more versatile competitor, trained to find a way forward no matter what.

You have to learn to stay calm in the face of troubles.

Look for the best way to help yourself and don't give in to fear or depression when you're at your weakest. Never accept a victim's mentality.

Answer the following questions as sincerely as you can

1. Working out is a good way to prepare for life itself because life is a grueling endurance sport. True **or** False
2. If you have challenges or issues that affect your primary passion, refocus your energy elsewhere. True **or** False
3. It's essential to work on your weakness so that when life plays a fast one on you, you can pour yourself into something else. Yes **or** No
4. Write out your daily routine and the time for each activity right after you wake up till you get in bed to sleep at night. If you stay up in the middle of the night, write it out too. An example: 2:15 am – 5:30 am: Awake watching Netflix; 7 am: wake up, and take my bath and have breakfast. Write it all down

_____

_____

_____

_____

_____

_____

_____

_____

_____

_____

_____

_____

_____

_____

5. Pick out the essential activities, the activities that serve as a distraction, and the non-important ones too. Create a table with three rows and label it as Essential, Distractions, and Non-important. (The non-important activities are activities that must be done, but they aren't a priority. An example is taking out the waste or cleaning the house. It's important, but you don't have to do it immediately, you wake up. Distractions are activities that wouldn't affect you if you don't do them. An example can be watching a movie or playing a game.)

Essential	Distraction	Non-important

6. Look through the essential activities and compare the time you spend with the essential to the time you spend with the distracting and non-important activities. When you do this, create a new time schedule for your essential activities. Make sure it includes meal breaks, and you don't sacrifice your sleep as it will affect productivity.
7. At the end of the week, evaluate your actions and your productivity. How effective were you after the first week? Did you do more? Was there a change in your attitude? Write it down

_____

_____

_____

_____

_____

_____

8. What were the obstacles that were in your way? How did you deal with it?

_____

_____

_____

_____

_____

_____

9. Look at one challenge that has constantly been in your way for a long time. It can be losing weight, learning a new language, studying, or saving up to buy a house or car. Create a work ethic for this challenge. It can be running a few miles before dawn to lose weight, taking long walks, or cutting expenses to save costs. Dedicate each hour to a particular task. Write out your work ethic.

_____

_____

_____

_____

_____

_____

10. Remember your cookie jar? Go through it and look for an astonishing challenge you've faced. Think about it and remember what you went through and how you got over it. Go on social media and write a post about it while using the hashtag #canthurtme #talentnotrequired

CHAPTER 9: UNCOMMON AGAINST UNCOMMON

Here are a few points we learned in this chapter

The uncommon among the uncommon doesn't take breaks.

No matter who you are, life will present you with similar opportunities where you can prove to be uncommon. You must be someone who refuses to ignore getting all duties done to be such an uncommon fellow. You don't have to be specially trained to be such a person; you simply need to want it and give all you've got like your life depends on it.

An uncommon among the uncommon would always raise the bar higher. Never let your desire for comfort rule you.

When becoming uncommon among uncommon, it is possible to push yourself to a place that is beyond the current capability or temporal mindset of the people you work with. However, this shouldn't give you a superior ego and don't lord yourself over the team because it wouldn't help you or your team members and your relationship with the team. This is important.

It is important to be at the same level with your teammates; this helps you to feel what they feel, you can understand what they are going through, and you make it easy for them to approach you.

Sometimes the only thing that can help you get through difficult situations from superiors is your ability to see the purpose of the training or challenge instead of listening to what they are saying about you. This is what determines what you do with the opportunities revoked or presented to you, and it also determines how your story plays out. If an opportunity is revoked, you may decide to get angry and give an attitude to anyone around you, but know you wouldn't go far with this attitude.

You don't need to accept defeat because things will definitely not go the way you intend it to go every time. You simply need to find the spot where you missed it or the last place where everything made sense to you before it got muddled up and find the right way from there. This way, you get better, and you can be sure your effort wouldn't go unnoticed.

Prejudice is everywhere. If you find yourself in a situation where it is used against you, the onus falls on you to decide how you're going to handle it. Let it fuel you by adding it to the resources that make your dreams come true, so it will make you believe in yourself. Trust me when I say it will make every challenge you come across more difficult, and this will, in turn, make your victory sweeter at the end.

Focus on what's important and not your mistakes

Answer the following questions as sincerely as you can

1. A true leader may not stay exhausted but must be strong.
   True **or** False
2. A true leader never looks down on the weakest link and will always shun arrogance. True **or** False
3. To be uncommon among the uncommon means being one of the best and helping your men find their best.
   True **or** False
4. Create a scenario that can help you become uncommon among the uncommon. It may be giving in double time at work, helping older citizens around you, running an extra mile, staying fit, or any situation at all. Don't think of a situation you can accomplish without struggle. Think of one scenario that's challenging, and people would have to look up to you.

   _____
   _____

5. Now create your daily routine for the task. Your daily routine will have to be consistent. If the scenario you created is about

cleaning up the environment, create your daily schedule that revolves around your task right from when you wake up till when you sleep. You may not have to spend your twenty-four hours carrying out the task, but your daily routine should revolve around it.

_____

_____

_____

_____

_____

_____

_____

_____

_____

_____

_____

_____

_____

_____

_____

_____

6. If you're a leader of a team, who enjoys their comfort zone and see no need to earn their reputation every day, how do you manage such a situation and encourage your team members to always be their best and, at the same time become someone they can trust? What do you do? Do you wake up early and do your part or do double tasks or encourage them with your words and actions? What would you do?

_____

_____

_____

_____

_____

_____

7. Imagine you have a teenager who is doing well as a leader, but her mind is only focused on getting the work done, and she doesn't see how it affects her teammates. How do you help her? What do you do to help her understand the importance of feedback and empathy? Do you encourage her to listen, or what would you do?

_____

_____

_____

_____

_____

_____

8. Explain a very difficult task you went through to your teenager. The story must include how you were made a member of a team, how you were treated, your mistakes, how you overcame, how you led the group, and what the teenager can learn from the story.

_____

_____

_____

_____

_____

_____

9. Imagine you are a rookie and the latest member of a team. You are supposed to stand out, but every member of your team has won medals at different times, and they will be too happy to pull you down. What do you do to prove yourself?

_____

_____

_____

_____

_____

_____

10. Write a note to your younger self explaining the contradictions and all you had to endure to get in the lead and what you would have done differently to become better. End the story with the hashtag #canthurtme #uncommonamongstuncommon.

CHAPTER 10: THE EMPOWERMENT OF FAILURE

Here are a few points we learned in this chapter

Let people's wrong opinions and motives about you remain what they are. The only time you should give it the access for it to matter to you is when you need it to fuel your resources and show to these people and the whole world they've got nothing on you.

It doesn't matter the grueling path you have to take when you need to succeed. It doesn't matter if you have to take a particular task, course, or class more than once; do it if you have to and ensure you win no matter who is or isn't watching.

Use your encouragements as your fuel and reason to move forward.

The thing about following the power supply is you'd better make sure you're on the right line.

Be conscious of your environment and what you do. It makes it easier for you to find your way back and rebound when you get lost or when you're off the track.

Always aim to be the best at whatever you do. If you are, people will notice you and take note of how good you are, and this will always come up to your own advantage. Never deliver a performance that is below your capacity.

It's great to push yourself beyond the limits that you know. However, you also have to learn to listen to your body, so you avoid a full break down. If you feel something unusual, visit your doctor early and don't wait till there's a major challenge or breakdown in your body before you see the doctor.

Never allow yourself to develop a quitter's mentality. If there's something you do because you like it or it's your passion, and it has become a part of your routine, enjoy it and give it all you've got. However, if you find out you can't participate in this task for any reason at all, you don't need to quit. You only need to find another passion or task that's as satisfying as the one you're used to.

Set new standards for yourself. If what you have to work with is something you don't like, create your own standards even if no one believes in what you're doing.

Giving up is never an option. Never surround yourself with people who speak to your desire for comfort.

Many of the battles we fight are won or lost in our heads; when we're in a foxhole we usually aren't alone, and we need to be confident in the quality of the heart, mind, and dialogue of the person hunkered down with us because at some point we need empowering and encouraging words to keep us focused and deadly.

Meltdowns in life are inevitable in life. However, meltdowns aren't as important as how you handle them. Never let it derail you or take over your mindset, sabotage your good relationships with people who are supposed to be your support team.

Don't bend to the whim of your every failure. Get up, dust yourself up, and keep moving forward.

Don't expect that you'll get lucky all the time because things will never always go the way you want it to go. If you feel entitled, cut it loose and don't focus on what you think you deserve. Focus on what you're willing to learn. This will eventually stretch and help your mind.

It's important to perform due diligence for every task. Check your mindset to see how committed you were as well as your preparation and determination levels. This helps you check your belief and reaffirm your resolve to the task at hand.

Life is a mind game. Realize it and own it.

Answer the following questions as sincerely as you can

1. You can't prepare for unknown factors, but if you have a better pre-game focus, you will likely only have to deal with one or two rather than ten. True **or** False

2. Showing no weakness doesn't mean you are strong.
   True **or** False

3. Most wars are won or lost in our own heads.
   True **or** False

4. In life, there's no gift as overlooked or inevitable as a failure.
   Yes **or** No

5. If you are in a situation where you find yourself knocked down and out, mention three people who would be there to support you or give you words of encouragement that uplift your soul.

   _____
   _____
   _____
   _____

6. Why did you pick them? Will they always tell you what you want to hear or will they look you in your face, tell you the truth and help you up? Explain your reasons

   _____
   _____
   _____
   _____
   _____
   _____

7. Mention 3 people who wouldn't tell you the truth in any situation but would tell you only words that you want to hear.

   _____
   _____
   _____

8. If you were on a show and you needed someone to save you, would you call any of the three of them? Yes **or** No
9. Would you want to be any of these 3 people? Yes **or** No
10. Take a quick look over your life. What was the biggest failure that affected you so much in life? How did this failure make you look dumb?

_____

_____

_____

_____

_____

_____

11. What did you learn from this mistake? How did you turn the situation around? Did you have help from your friends, family, teammates, or support team? How did you get over it?

_____

_____

_____

_____

_____

_____

12. What is the ratio of your luck versus your failures for different tasks? Is it Luck 7 and Failures 3 or luck 2 and failures 8?

_____

_____

13. Imagine your 10-year-old son was made the lead of his science group or boys scout, and he made plans of how everything would go smoothly without a hitch while basing most of his belief on luck. How do you help him find his balance in a realistic way?

_____

_____

_____

_____

_____

_____

14. Have you ever listened to the voice of superiors or professionals over your inner voice and beliefs?
Yes **or** No

15. How did the situation turn out in the end? Was it a disaster? Did you have regrets at the end? Did you build your esteem and help your beliefs? Write down how you felt afterward.

_____

_____

_____

_____

_____

_____

16. Take out your journal and write out words to boost your confidence and tear down your doubts. Write them on sticky notes and place them on your accountability mirror, your refrigerator, your bedside, and places where you can easily see them. Here's an example: I can accomplish every task before me, no matter what people say or think.

_____

_____

_____

_____

_____

_____

17. Your daughter comes knocking your door at 3 am with tears and fear streaming down her face. She has been made the leader of the science team in her class, and the team would be competing with other teams from other schools. She needs a strategy. Draw one with her.

_____

_____

_____

_____

_____

_____

18. Think about your recent success story. Write all about the experience from the preparation to the training, execution and everything on social media with the hashtag #canthurtme #empowermentoffailure

CHAPTER 11: WHAT IF?

Here are a few points we learned in this chapter

Keep your eyes and mind open to watch the people around you. Watch and learn what makes them excel.

Find what works for you. Psychologists say it takes sixty-six days for some people to build a habit, but it may take a lesser or longer time for you to learn. Never stop learning; always find ways to grow and become better.

You can grow upbeat down, abused, uneducated, rejected, abandoned, and unhealthy, but it still takes you to decide how your life goes.

No matter what happens, never feel sorry for yourself. Have an attitude of gratitude always. Be gentle with yourself and take time to relax and have fun. Never dwell on rage.

Live your life and love your life. Never be too hard on yourself. Appreciate the people who matter to you and let them know it.

When you push beyond your perceived capability, your mind won't stop thinking about it. This is a way to send you into panic and doubt, which heightens your self-torture. However, breaking past that point of pain saturates the mind so you can become single-pointed. This will push your boundaries and help you connect with yourself to the deepest part of your soul. This helps you realize yourself.

Find what works for you; don't live on what everyone else says. Never give up without a fight.

You can't stop your brain and mind from visualizing self-doubt, but you can neutralize it and other external chatter by asking *What If*. *What If* is the power and permission to face down your darkest demons, your worst memories and accept them as part of your history. If and when you do that, you'll be able to use them as fuel to envision the most audacious, outrageous achievement and go get it.

Answer the following questions as sincerely as you can

1. In life, there are countless trails to self-realization, and you can come into this realization through grueling and intense discipline True **or** False
2. It's not the external voice but what you tell yourself that matters. True **or** False
3. Self-doubt is a natural reaction to any bold attempt to change your life for the better. True **or** False
4. What conditions and variables can pull you down real quick? Is it the weather, hurt, doubt, or pain? Mention them

_____

_____

_____

_____

_____

_____

5. Are there a few people you know that do the same things you do and inspire you? Yes **or** No
6. If your answer is yes, why do they inspire you? Mention three of them and what you've learned from them.

_____

_____

_____

_____

_____

_____

7. Write something about how they've inspired you and how you appreciate them and send it to them. You can send a gift to them as well.

_____

_____

8. You meet a teenager who grew up under the worst circumstances, and she feels like her life is over, and she can't be productive. How can you help her? What do you say to her?

_____

_____

_____

_____

_____

_____

9. When you need to make decisions, what are the factors you consider first? Is it money, your abilities, your health, your fears, the worrying voice inside your head, those around you, or your parents? Mention them

_____

_____

_____

_____

_____

_____

10. Mention the top ten things you appreciate about yourself and the reason why you do. Place it on your accountability mirror.

_____

_____

_____

_____

_____

_____

_____

_____

_____

_____

_____

_____

_____

_____

_____

11. Mention five things you do for fun

_____

_____

_____

_____

_____

_____

_____

12. Do you judge yourself? Do you get hard on yourself?
    Yes **or** No
13. What are your reasons for being too hard on yourself? Do you
    think that's what will make you become better or you have no
    reason at all? Pen it down

_____

_____

_____

_____

_____

_____

_____

14. If your child also judged himself for the same reasons, what would you say to him?

_____

_____

_____

_____

_____

_____

_____

_____

15. What is your daily routine for intense discipline and self-realization? Is it meditation, prayer, yoga, jogging, or running? Mention them.

_____

_____

_____

_____

_____

_____

Made in the USA
Las Vegas, NV
16 March 2021